I0559480

My First Cute
Farm Animals
Dot Marker Coloring Book

for Kids Ages 1-5

Bold and Easy Guided Big Fill the Dots for Early Learning | Fun Activity & Craft Sheets to Boost Creativity and Fine Motor Skills | Perfect Gift for Toddlers and Preschoolers

POLYMATH
Panda

ISBN: 978-1-953149-81-7
Copyright © 2024 by Polymath Panda

This Book Belongs To:

_____

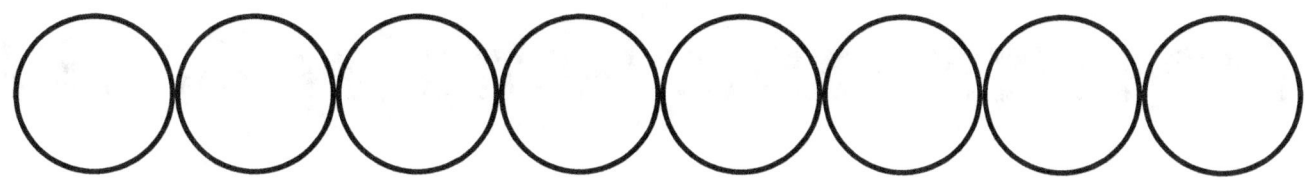

Grab Your Dot Markers and Dive into 50 Fun-Filled Pages of Cows, Chickens, and many more!

Featuring a wide variety of Farm animals including Horse, Sheep, Chicken, Pig, Goats, and more. Includes engaging activities like I Spy, Counting, Mazes, Color Matching, and Scissor Cutting, all designed with large, easy-to-color dots. Perfectly compatible with all leading dot marker brands with consistent 0.75 inch (18mm) dots.

This book is a fantastic fit for young explorers aged 1 - 5. It's crafted to enhance your child's early learning journey with delightful farm animals designs that connect words, images, and colors. Our team of skilled designers has ensured each page stimulates your child's imagination and helps build their fine motor skills, making learning an exciting adventure!

We understand the enthusiasm of young dot marker artists, so we've designed each page to be single-sided, minimizing the risk of colors bleeding through. Additionally, placing a sheet of paper or card between the pages can be a great way to keep everything tidy!

Thank you for choosing this book! We hope it brings you and your child countless hours of dot marker joy and learning.

Free Printable Activity Book!

- **Ignites Imagination:** Coloring with a story helps kids picture scenes and boost creativity.
- **Boosts Reading:** Following the story while coloring improves reading skills naturally.
- **Enhances Focus:** Storytelling with coloring keeps kids engaged and builds concentration.
- **Fosters Connection:** Coloring helps kids emotionally bond with characters and plots.
- **Fun Learning:** Makes learning enjoyable and easy through playful coloring.

QR Code in the Back of the Book

Enjoying this Book?

We'd love to hear your thoughts

We may just send you something special.

Week 1

Horse

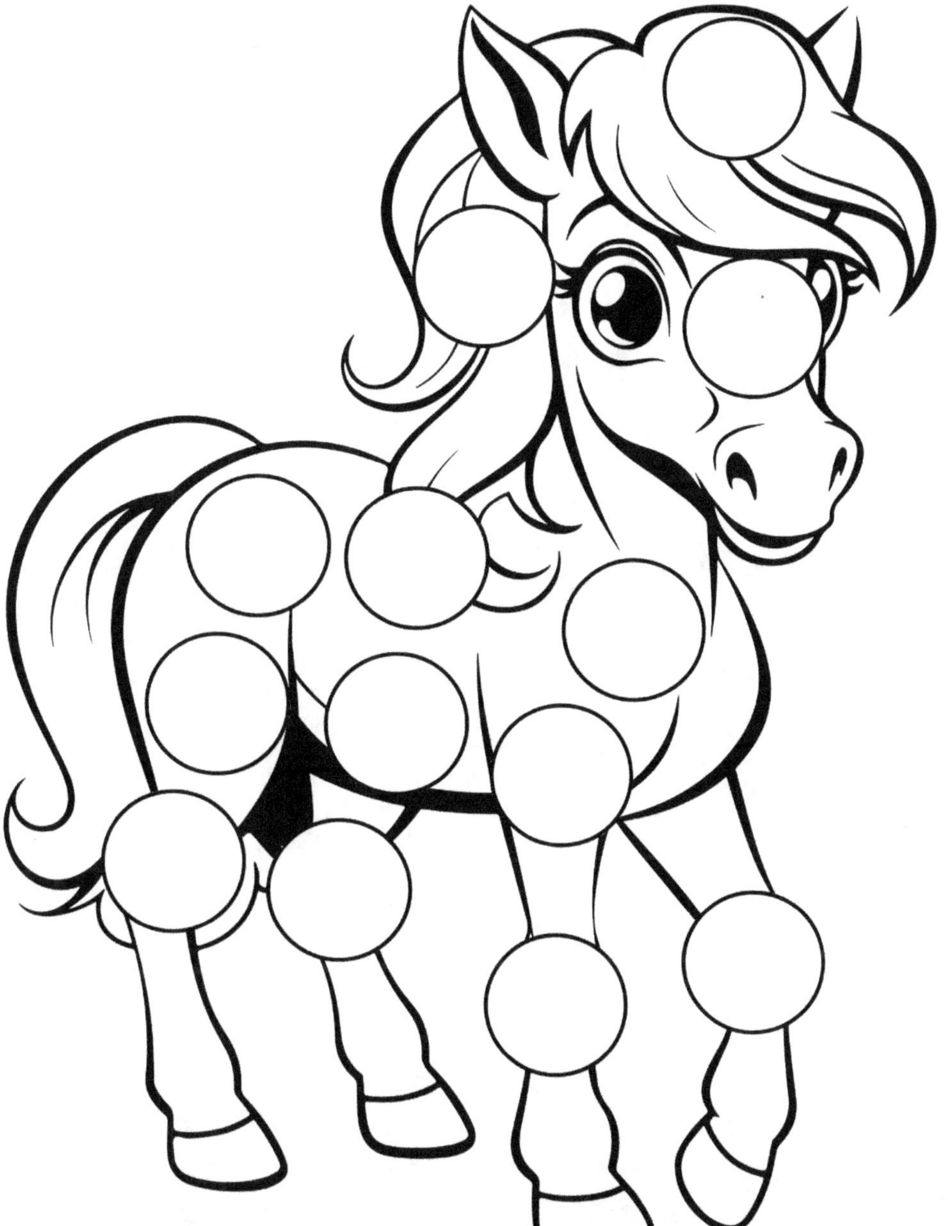

Spell out "Horse" by dotting each letter

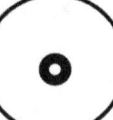

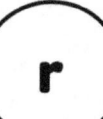

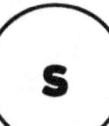

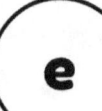

H o r s e

Scissor Practice

Cut along the dotted line to practice your scissor skills.

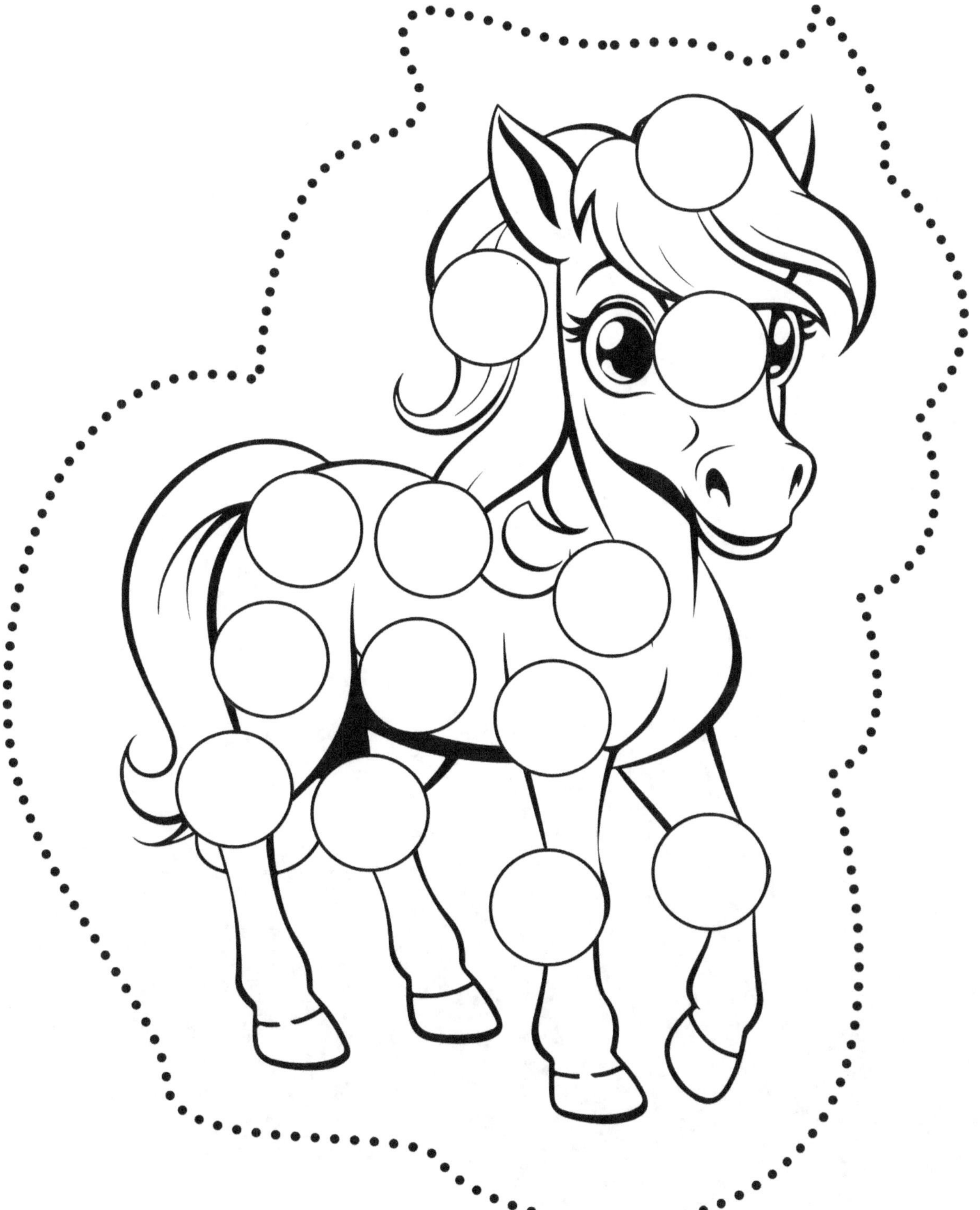

I Spy

I SPY **Find the Horse and dot it.**

Maze

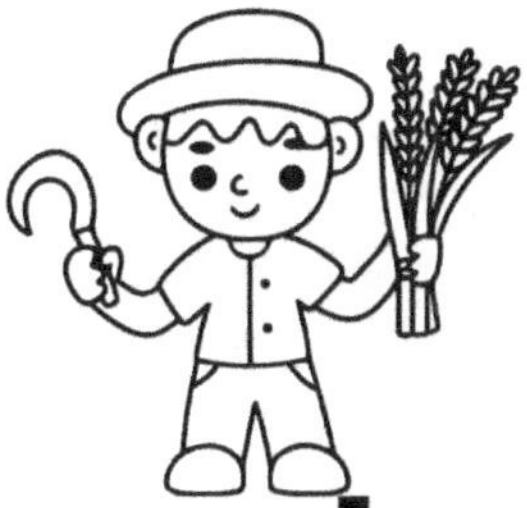

Dot the circles to help the farmer find the horse.

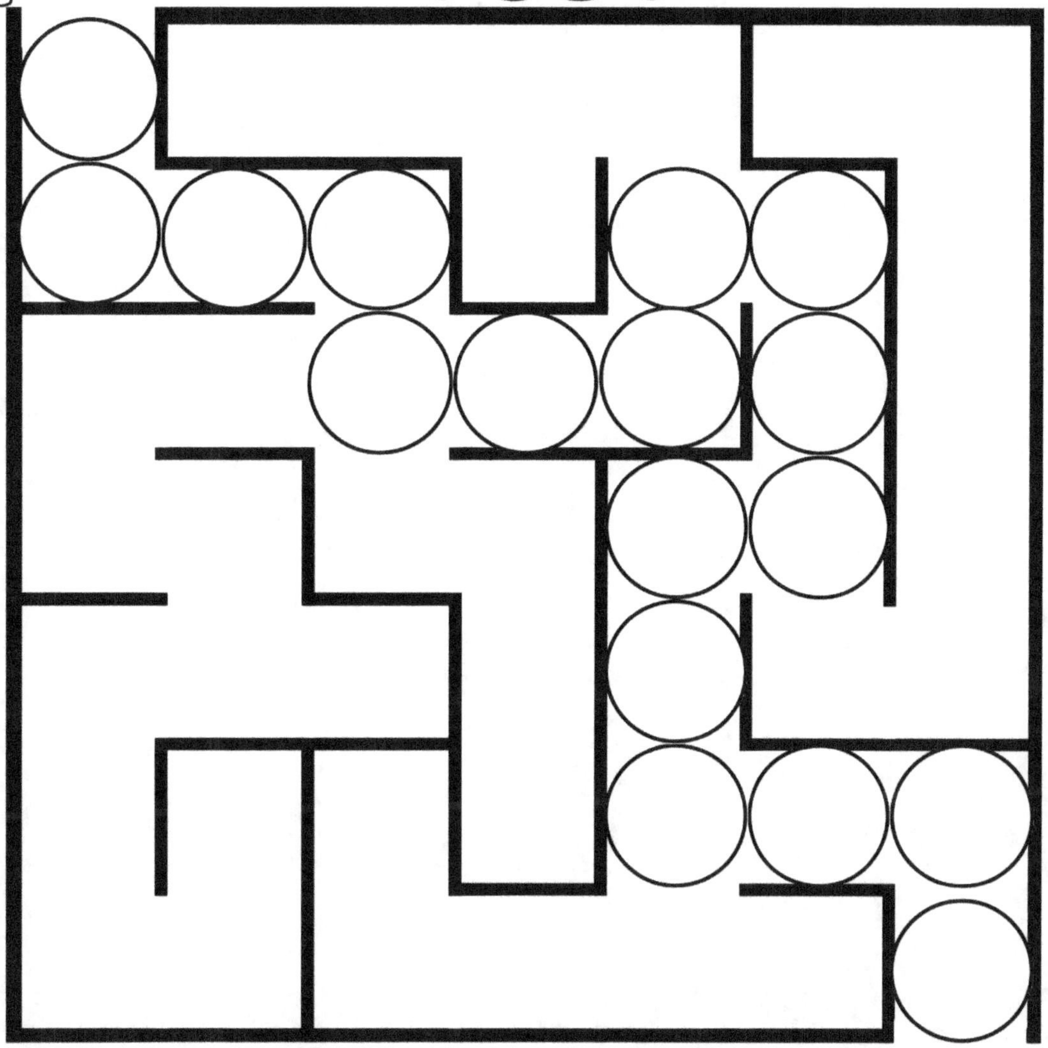

Great job!
The farmer found the horse!

Week 2

Cow

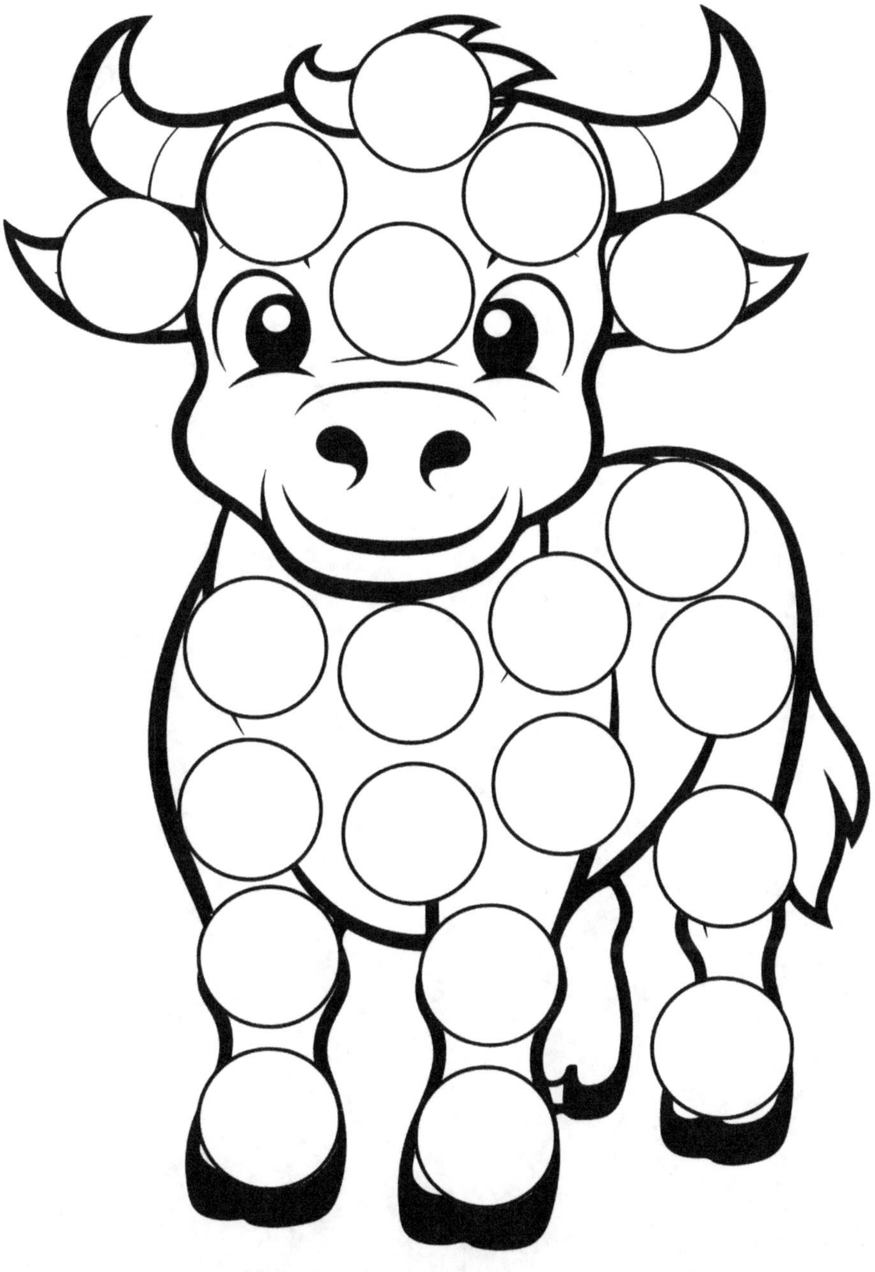

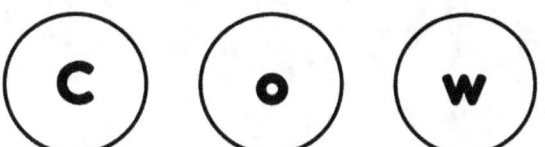

Spell out "Cow" by dotting each letter

C o w

Week 2

Scissor Practice

Cut along the dotted line to practice your scissor skills.

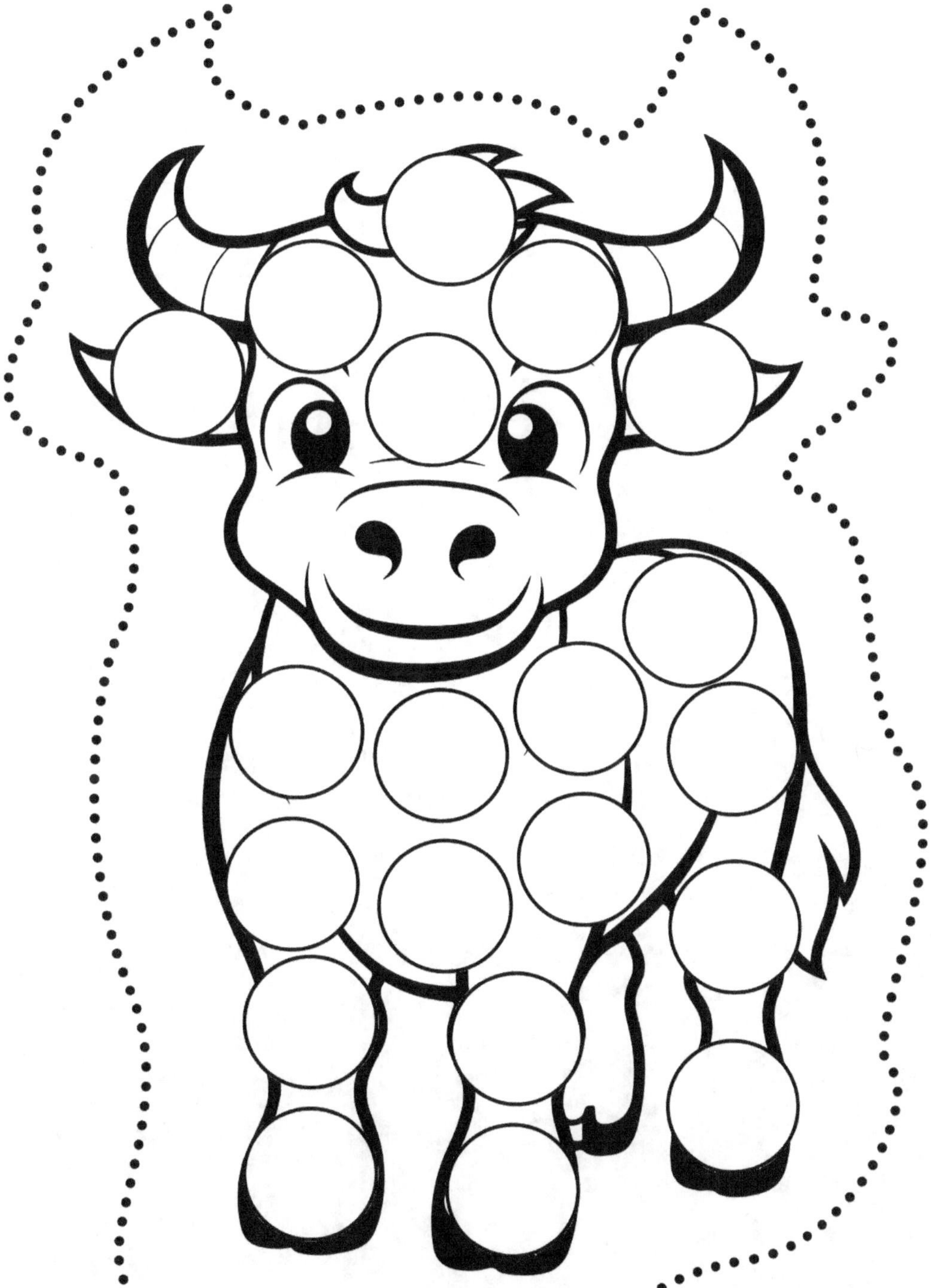

Week 2

Color Match

Dot all Cows Red

Dot all Horses Blue

Counting

Dot 3 Cows

Dot 2 Horses

Chicken

Spell out "Chicken" by dotting each letter

(C) (h) (i) (c) (k) (e) (n)

Week 3

Scissor Practice

Cut along the dotted line to practice your scissor skills.

10

Week 3

I Spy

I SPY   **Find the Chicken and dot it.**

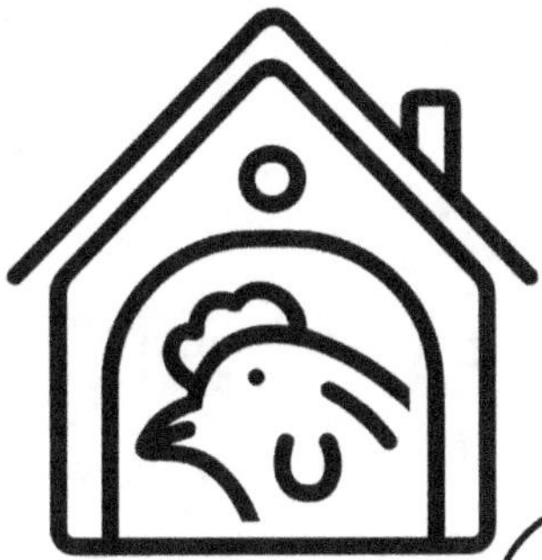

Fantastic!
The chicken found its home!

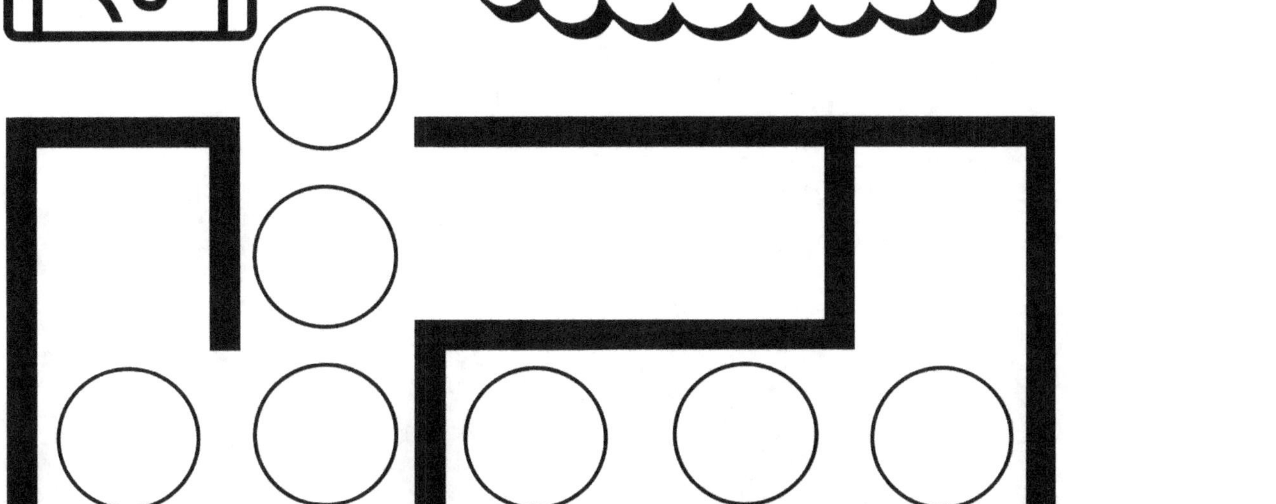

Dot the circles to help
the chicken find its home!

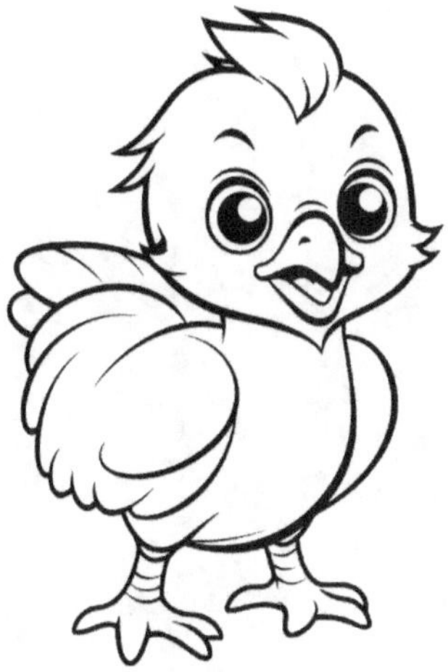

Goat

Spell out "Goat" by dotting each letter

 G    o    a    t

Week 4

Scissor Practice

Cut along the dotted line to practice your scissor skills.

14

Color Match

Dot all Chickens Violet ...... **Dot all Goats Orange**

Dot 4 Goats

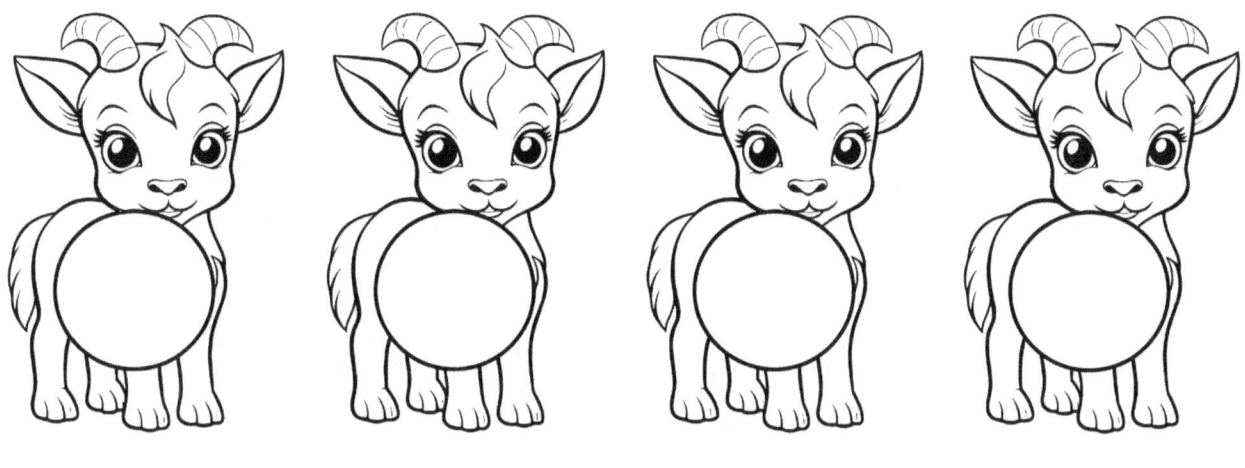

Dot 3 Chickens

Pig

Spell out "Pig" by dotting each letter

(P)   (i)   (g)

Week 5

Scissor Practice

Cut along the dotted line to practice your scissor skills.

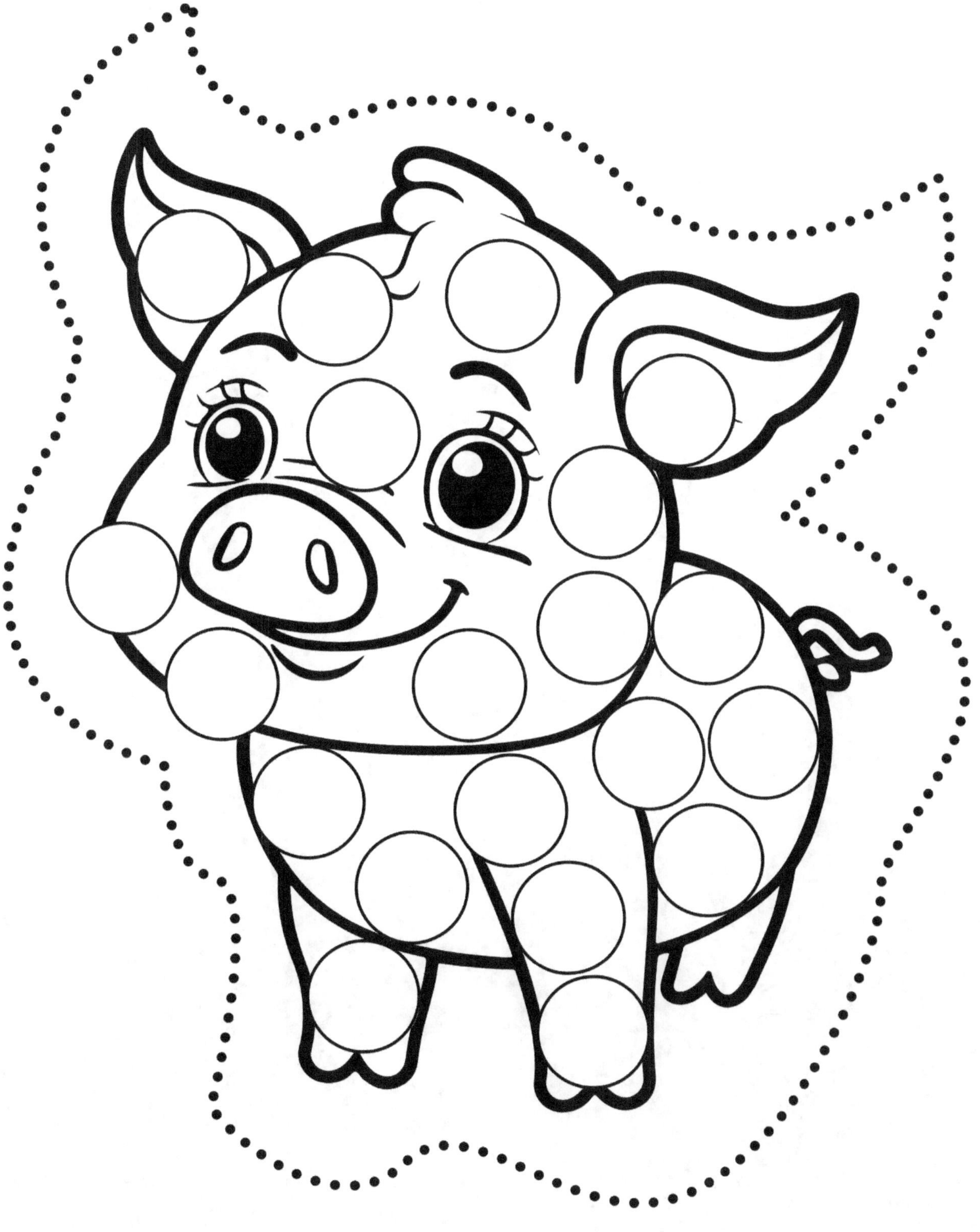

I Spy

I SPY **Find the Pig and dot it.**

Week 5

Maze

• •

Nicely done!
The pig found the muddy puddle!

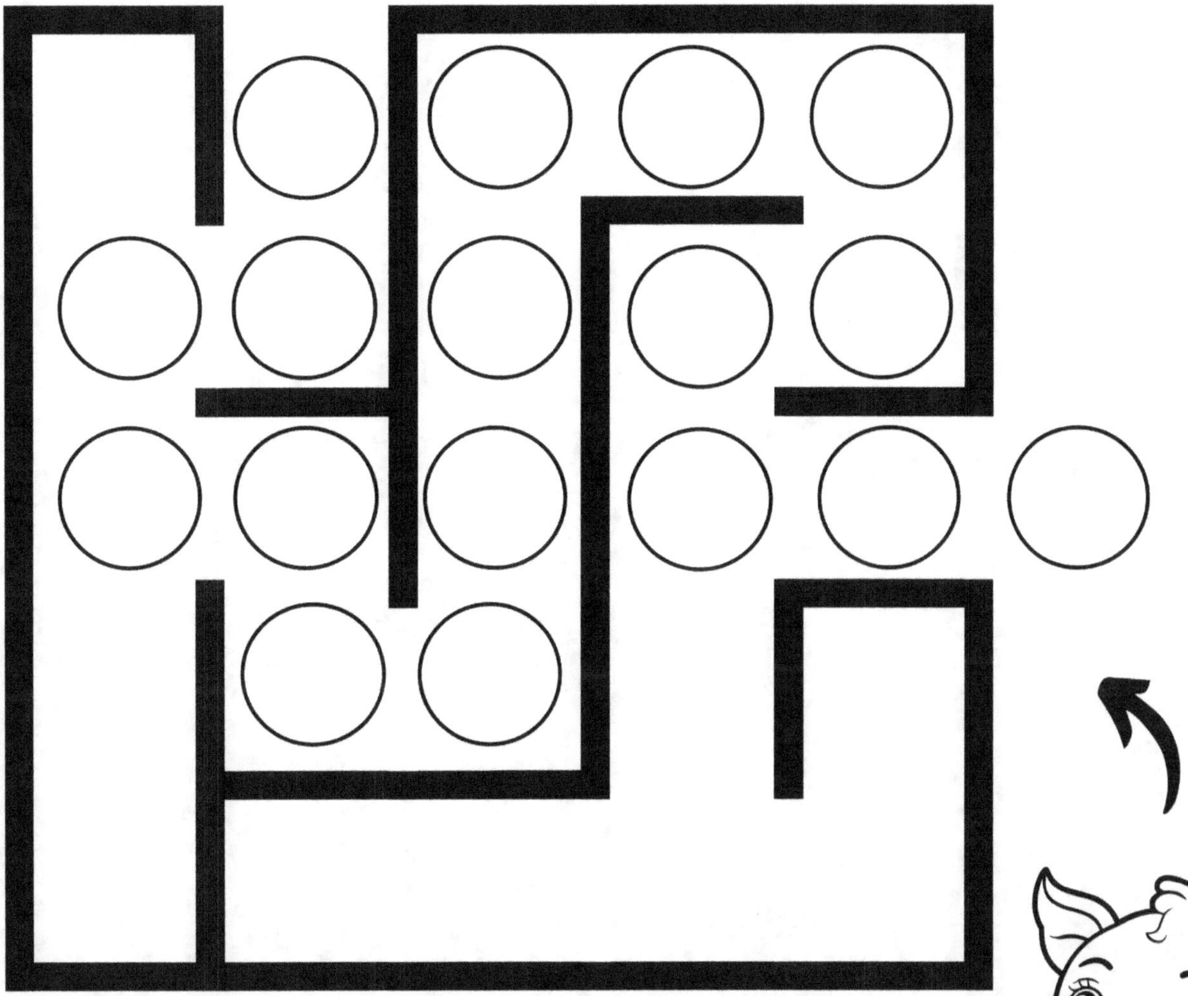

Dot the circles to help
the pig find the muddy puddle!

20

Duck

Spell out "Duck" by dotting each letter

D   u   c   k

Week 6

Scissor Practice

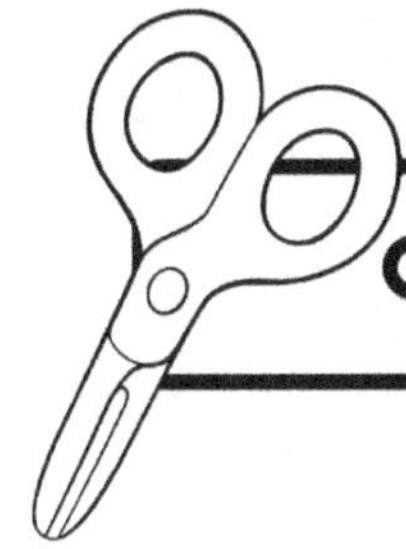

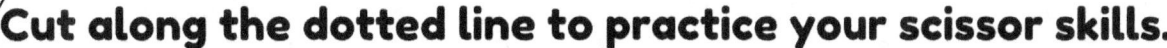

Cut along the dotted line to practice your scissor skills.

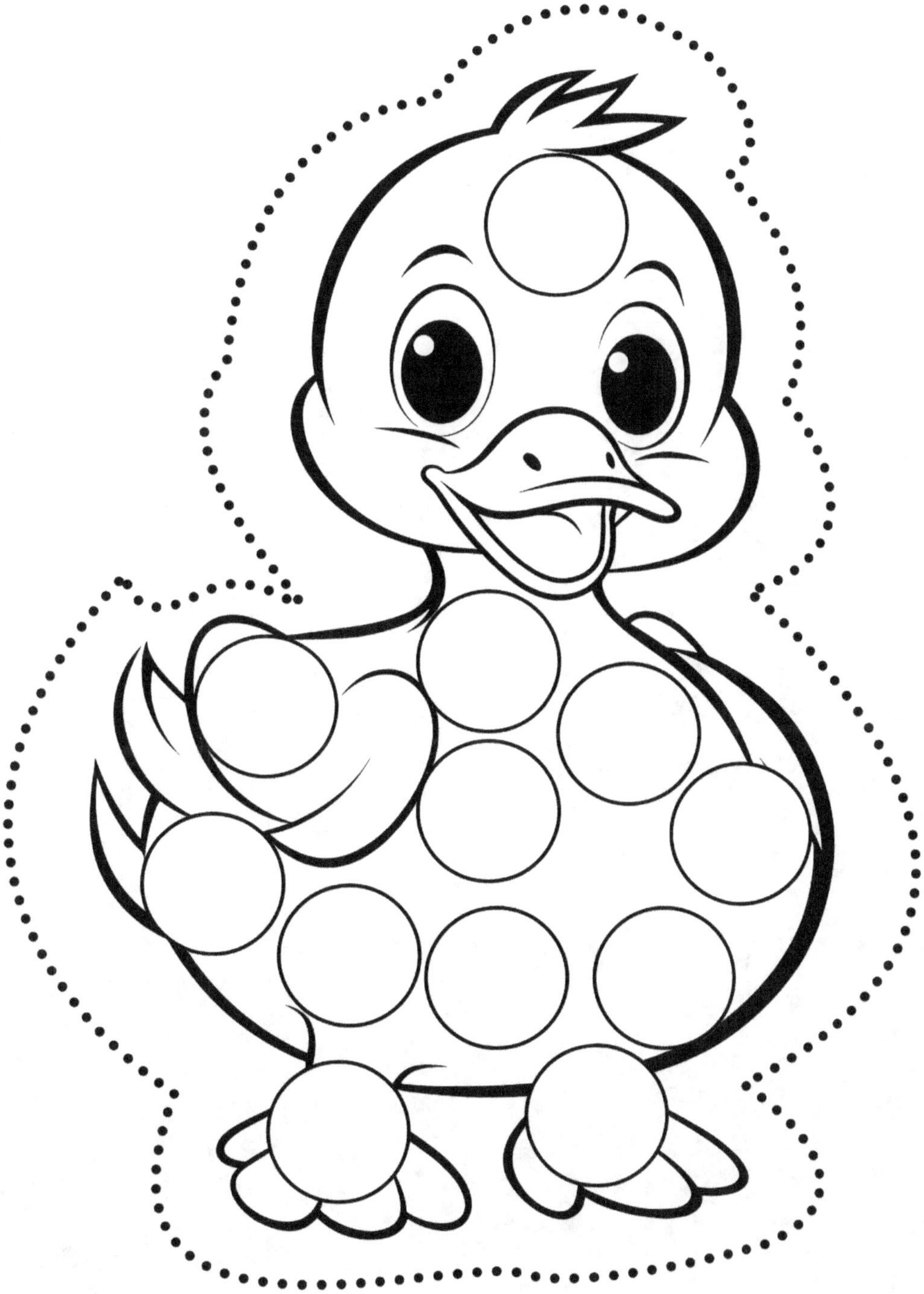

Dot all Pigs Orange

Dot all Ducks Blue

Counting

Dot 1 Pig

Dot 2 Ducks

Donkey

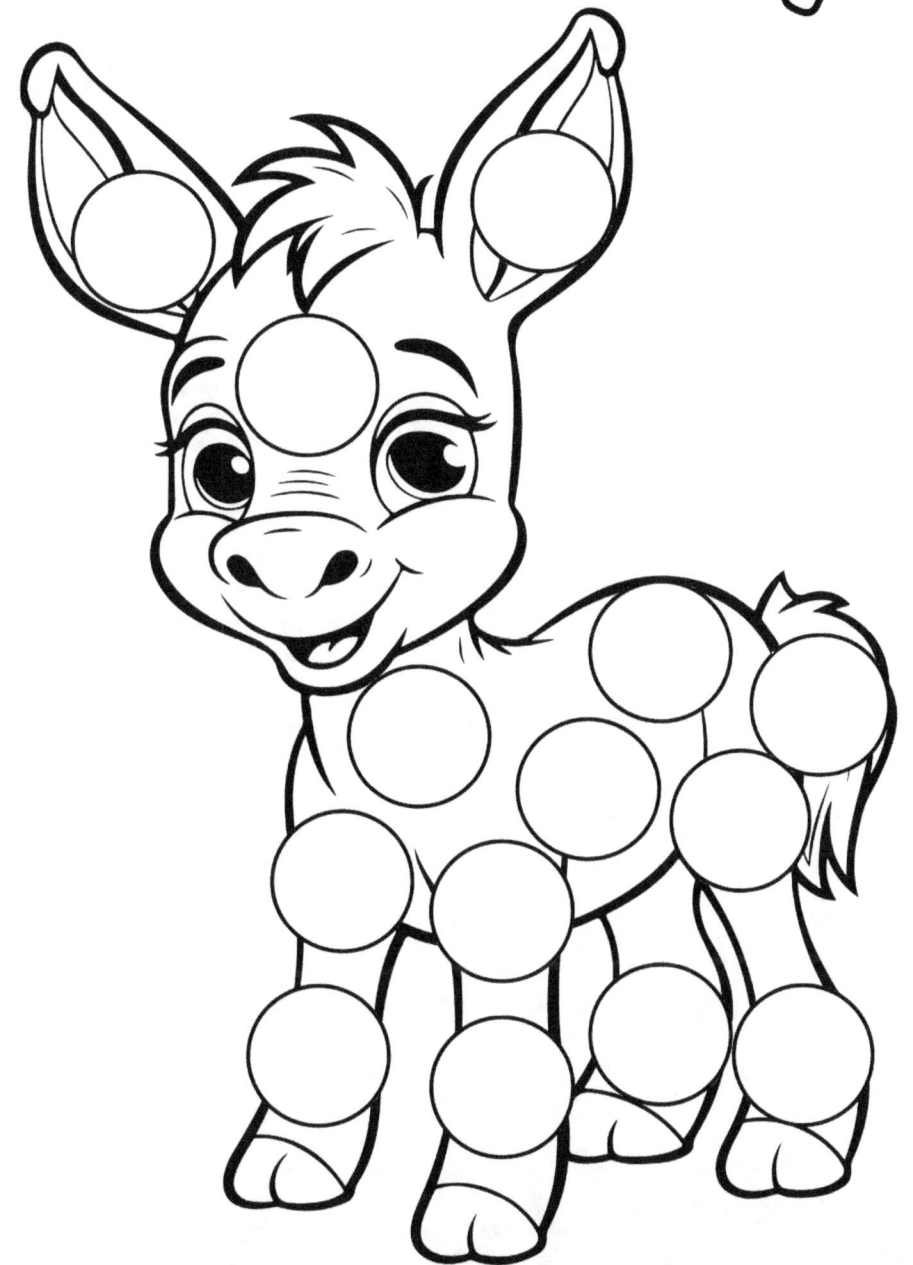

Spell out "Donkey" by dotting each letter

D   o   n   k   e   y

Week 7

Scissor Practice

Cut along the dotted line to practice your scissor skills.

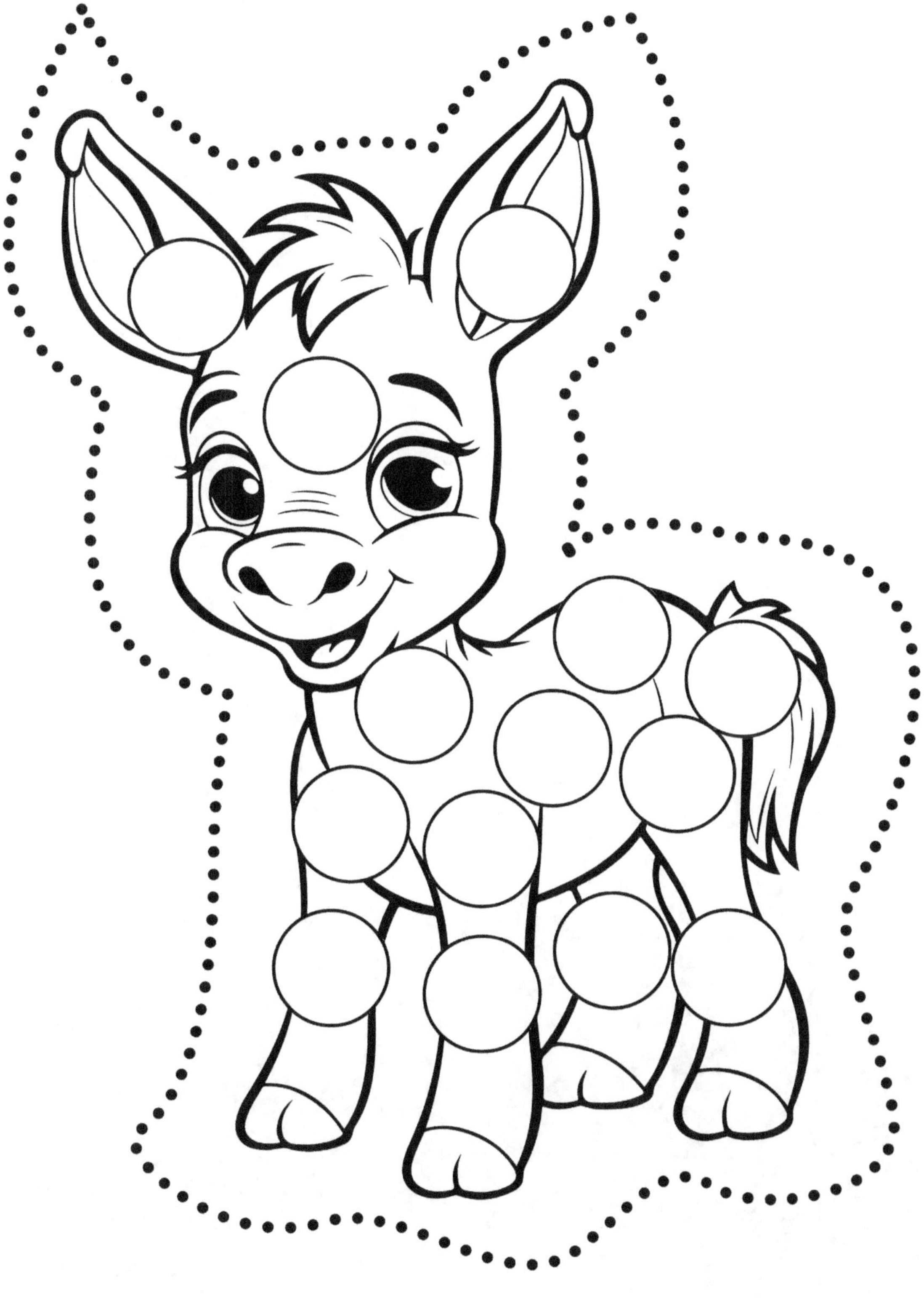

I Spy

I SPY   **Find the Donkey and dot it.**

Maze

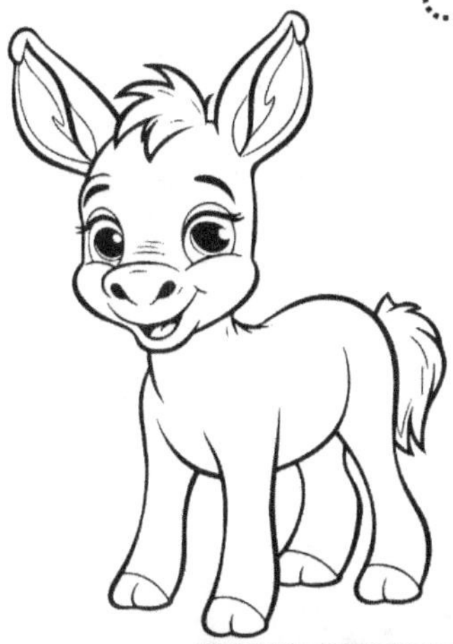

Dot the circles to help
The donkey find its hay.

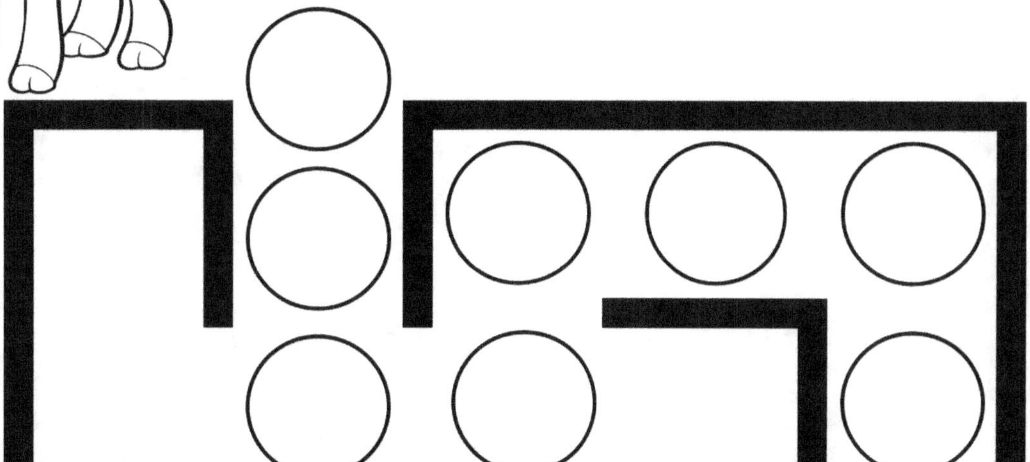

Awesome!
The donkey found its hay!

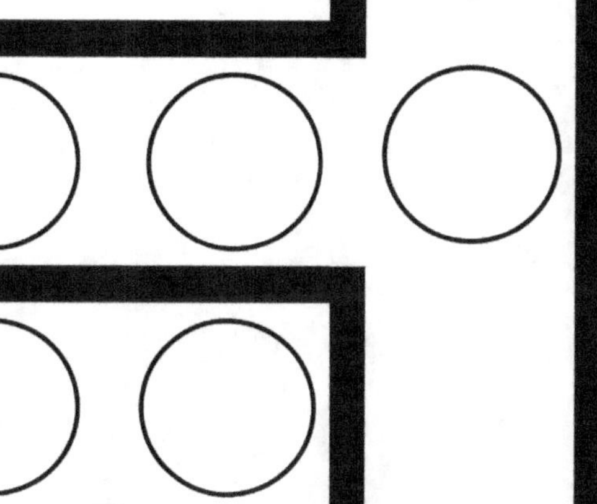

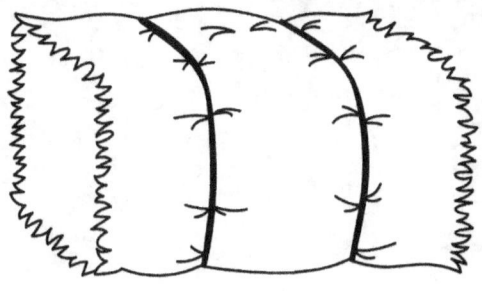

Alpaca

Spell out "Alpaca" by dotting each letter

(A) (A) (l) (p) (a) (c) (a)

Scissor Practice

Cut along the dotted line to practice your scissor skills.

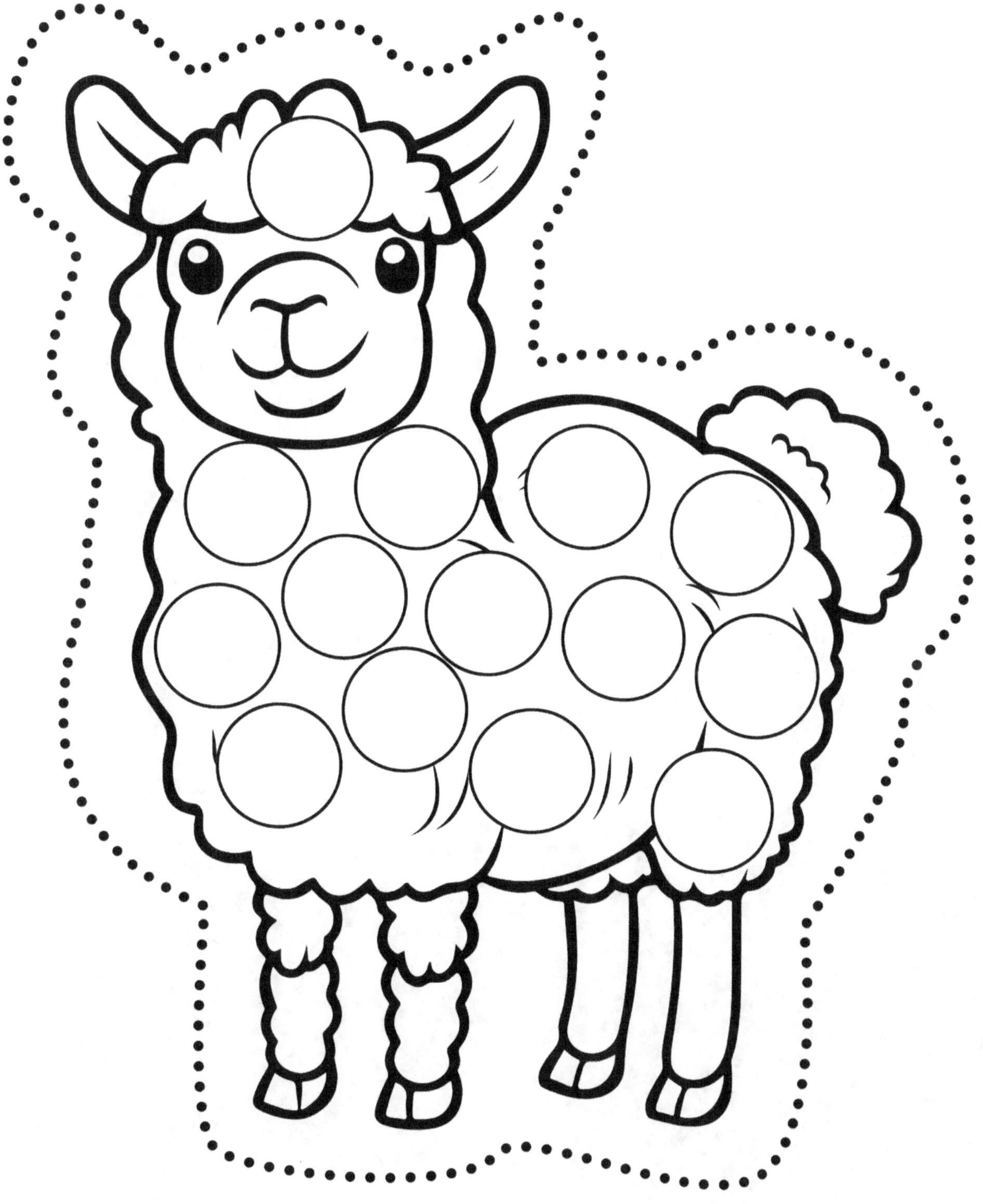

Color Match

Dot all Donkeys Green   Dot all Alpacas Red

Counting

Dot 2 Donkeys

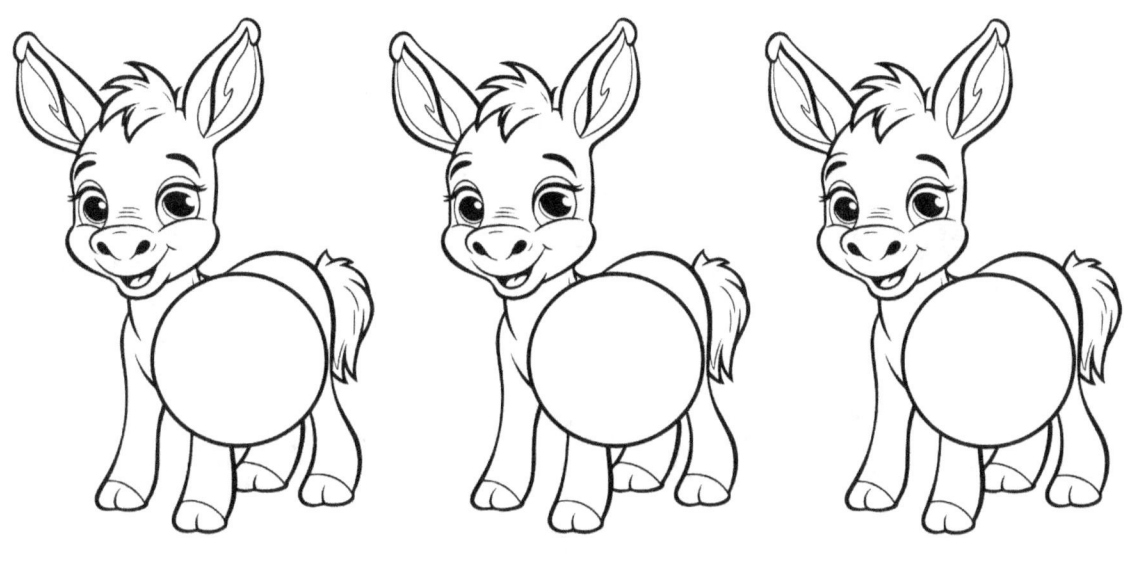

Dot 4 Alpacas

Sheep

Spell out "Sheep" by dotting each letter

(S) (h) (e) (e) (p)

Week 9

Scissor Practice

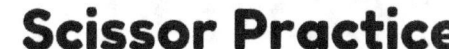

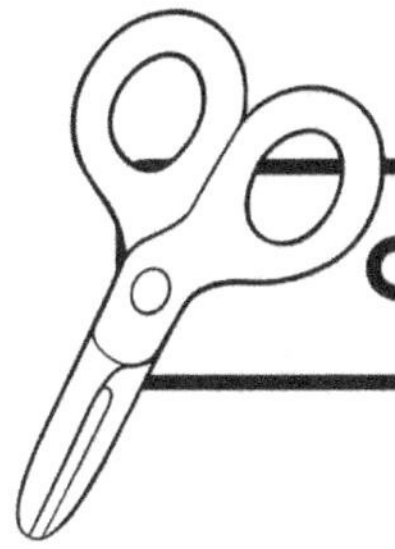

Cut along the dotted line to practice your scissor skills.

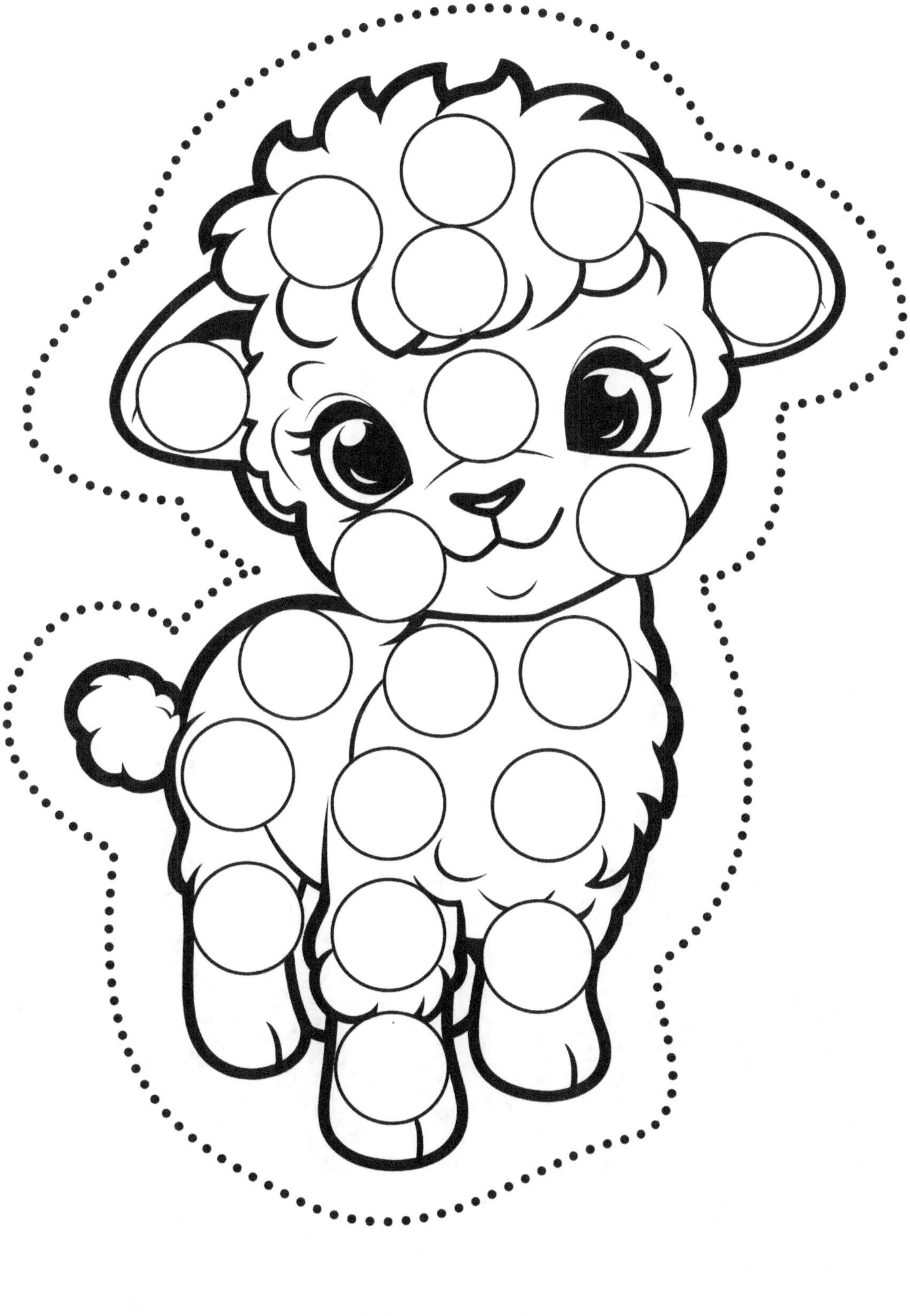

I Spy

I SPY **Find the Sheep and dot it.**

Well done!
The sheep found the grass!

Dot the circles to help
the sheep find the grass!

Camel

Spell out "Camel" by dotting each letter

C   a   m   e   l

Week 10

Scissor Practice

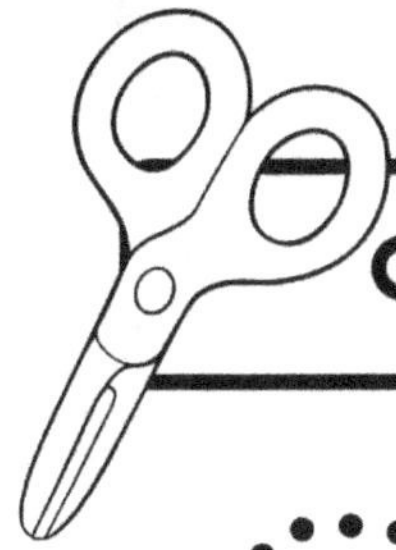

Cut along the dotted line to practice your scissor skills.

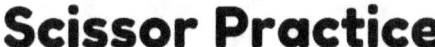

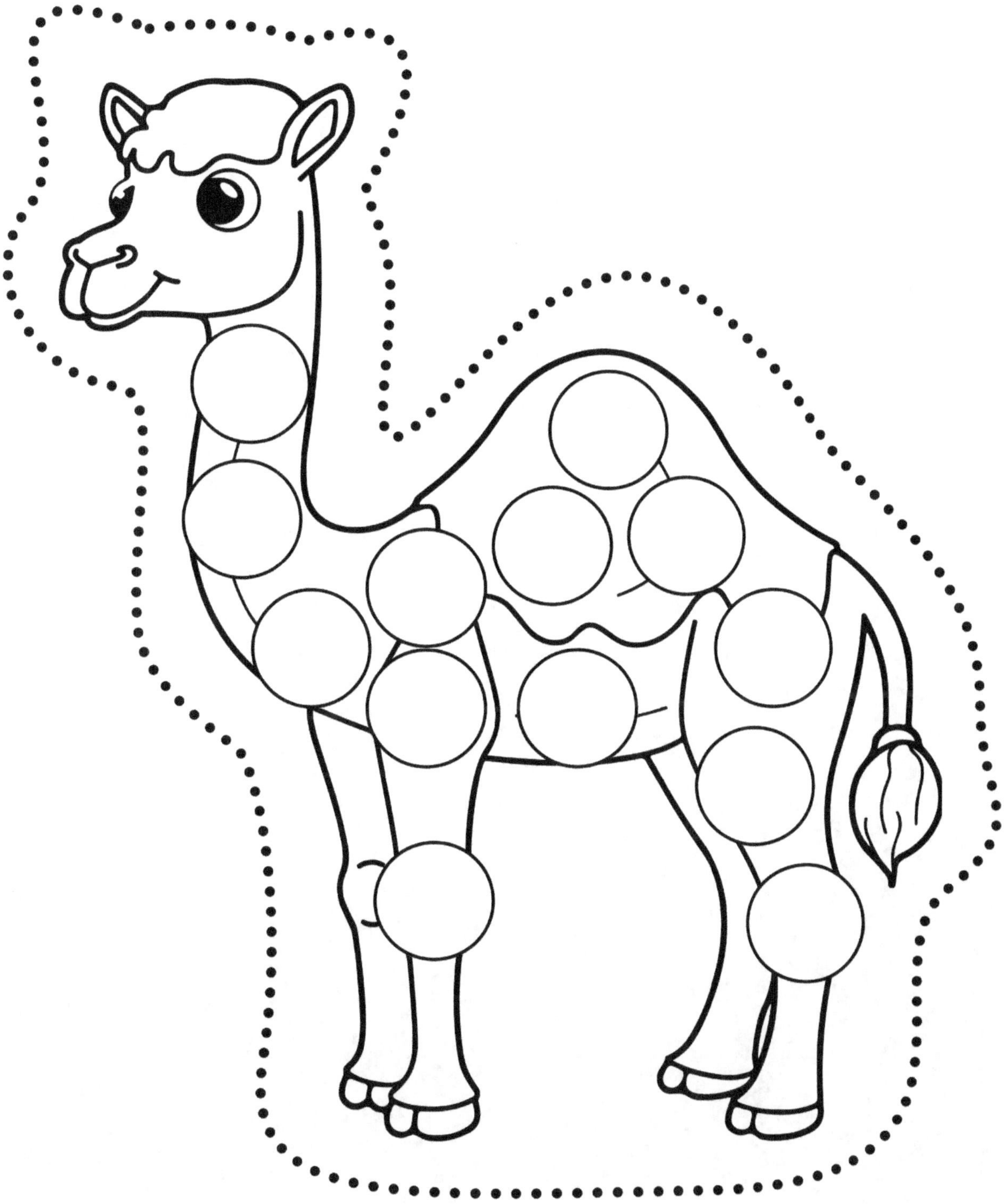

Color Match

Dot all Sheeps Yellow

Dot all Camels Orange

Counting

Dot 4 Sheeps

Dot 2 Camels

Bird

Spell out "Bird" by dotting each letter

B   i   r   d

Scissor Practice

Cut along the dotted line to practice your scissor skills.

I Spy

 **Find the Bird and dot it.**

Maze

Dot the circles to help
The bird find its nest.

Great!
The bird found its nest!

Rabbit

Spell out "Rabbit" by dotting each letter

(R) (a) (b) (b) (i) (t)

Scissor Practice

Cut along the dotted line to practice your scissor skills.

Week 12

Color Match

 Dot all Birds Orange

 Dot all Rabbits Green

47

Counting

Dot 4 Birds

Dot 1 Rabbit

Turkey

Spell out "Turkey" by dotting each letter

(T)   (u)   (r)   (k)   (e)   (y)

Scissor Practice

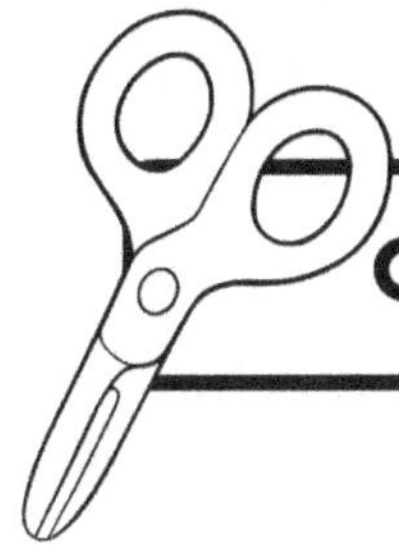

Cut along the dotted line to practice your scissor skills.

I Spy

I SPY   **Find the turkey and dot it.**

Maze

Dot the circles to help
The turkey find the berries.

Great!
The turkey found the berries!

Free Printable Activity Book!

- **Ignites Imagination:** Coloring with a story helps kids picture scenes and boost creativity.
- **Boosts Reading:** Following the story while coloring improves reading skills naturally.
- **Enhances Focus:** Storytelling with coloring keeps kids engaged and builds concentration.
- **Fosters Connection:** Coloring helps kids emotionally bond with characters and plots.
- **Fun Learning:** Makes learning enjoyable and easy through playful coloring.

Parents & Teachers!

Our biggest joy comes from helping little ones flourish and discover the world around them through learning.

That's why your thoughts matter so much to us!

Your honest thoughts about our book, even a quick sentence or two, would mean the world. We really mean it!

You'd be making a big difference for a small education brand like ours, run with love by a mother-daughter team.

Your reviews help us reach more curious minds across the globe, paving their way to success in their educational journey.

And hey, maybe we'll even sell a few more books in the process!

Every single review makes our hearts swell with gratitude.

Ready to make our day?

Scan the QR Code below to share your thoughts.

www.ingramcontent.com/pod-product-compliance
Lightning Source LLC
Chambersburg PA
CBHW081004120626
46546CB00010B/3010